Why Does a Mirror Show Things Backwards?

And other questions about LIGHT

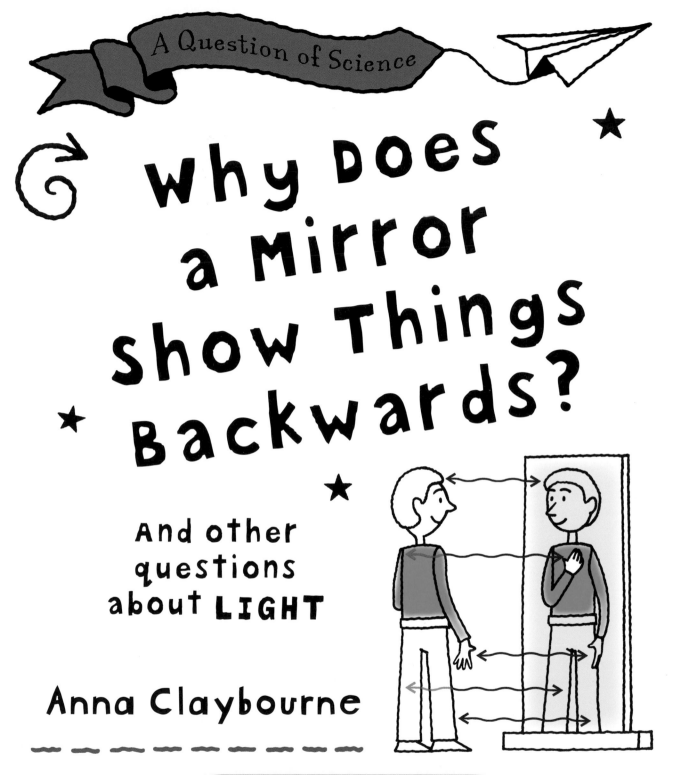

Anna Claybourne

CRABTREE
PUBLISHING COMPANY
WWW.CRABTREEBOOKS.COM

CRABTREE
PUBLISHING COMPANY
WWW.CRABTREEBOOKS.COM

Published in Canada
Crabtree Publishing
616 Welland Ave.
St. Catharines, Ontario
L2M 5V6

Published in the United States
Crabtree Publishing
347 Fifth Avenue
Suite 1402–145
New York, NY 10016

Published in 2021 by Crabtree Publishing Company

First published in 2020 by Wayland
© Hodder and Stoughton 2020

Author: Anna Claybourne

Editorial Director: Kathy Middleton

Editor: Julia Bird

Proofreader: Petrice Custance

Design and illustration: Matt Lilly

Cover design: Matt Lilly

Production coordinator and
 Prepress technician: Tammy McGarr

Print coordinator: Katherine Berti

Printed in the U.S.A./082020/CG20200601

Library and Achives Canada Cataloguing in Publication

Title: Why does a mirror show things backwards? : and other questions about light / Anna Claybourne.
Names: Claybourne, Anna, author.
Description: Series statement: A question of science | Includes index.
Identifiers: Canadiana (print) 20200254774 | Canadiana (ebook) 20200254790 | ISBN 9780778779094 (softcover) | ISBN 9780778777090 (hardcover) | ISBN 9781427125415 (HTML)
Subjects: LCSH: Light—Juvenile literature. | LCSH: Light—Miscellanea—Juvenile literature. | LCGFT: Trivia and miscellanea.
Classification: LCC QC360 .C53 2020 | DDC j535—dc23

Library of Congress Cataloging-in-Publication Data

Names: Claybourne, Anna, author.
Title: Why does a mirror show things backwards? : and other questions about light / Anna Claybourne.
Description: New York, NY : Crabtree Publishing Company, 2021. | Series: A question of science | First published in 2020 by Wayland.
Identifiers: LCCN 2020023420 (print) | LCCN 2020023421 (ebook) | ISBN 9780778777090 (hardcover) | ISBN 9780778779094 (paperback) | ISBN 9781427125415 (ebook)
Subjects: LCSH: Light--Juvenile literature.
Classification: LCC QC360 .C5687 2021 (print) | LCC QC360 (ebook) | DDC 535--dc23
LC record available at https://lccn.loc.gov/2020023420
LC ebook record available at https://lccn.loc.gov/2020023421

Contents

What is light?

Light is a type of **energy**. Examples of energy include heat, sound, movement, and electricity.

Weird energy

Light is a type of energy with some unusual features. Most forms of energy are invisible to humans. But we can sense light with our eyes.

We can see light from the stars even though they are trillions of miles away.

Where does light come from?

Light shines or glows from light sources:

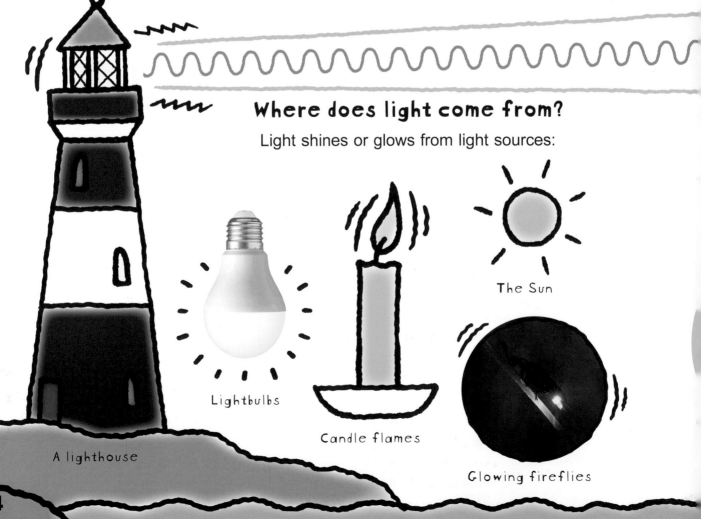

A lighthouse

Lightbulbs

Candle flames

The Sun

Glowing fireflies

Energy can't be made out of other materials. It can only come from changing one type of energy into another.

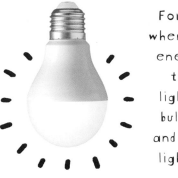

For example, when electrical energy flows through a lightbulb, the bulb heats up and glows with light energy.

Candle wax is a store of **chemical** energy. Light energy is made by burning the wax.

 ## Rays of light

Light zooms out from a light source in the form of rays or beams of light. This picture shows what's happening, but you don't actually see separate **light rays** and waves like this. You just see a glow, or an object with light shining from it.

Light rays travel in straight lines.

Light moves as a type of wave, called an **electromagnetic wave**.

Mysteries of light

Light is really quite weird. Check out these curious facts:

In some experiments, light clearly seems to be a wave. But in others, it acts more like a stream of little pockets of energy. Scientists call them photons.

Strong gravity can bend light— but no one is sure how!

Light is the fastest thing in the universe. Nothing can go faster.

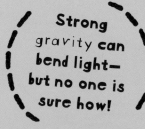

CAN'T BEAT ME!

Confused? You're not the only one! Scientists are still studying light and trying to find out more about it. But there are a few questions we can answer...so read on!

Where does light go when you turn it off?

GOOD NIGHT!

When you turn your bedroom light off at bedtime, the room goes dark. That's convenient, otherwise you couldn't get to sleep!

But where does the light actually go? Shouldn't all that light energy still be bouncing around inside your room and lighting it up?

YES!

This does actually happen, but it lasts such a short time that you can't see it. Light just travels too mindbogglingly fast.

Light does reflect, or bounce off, objects. That's what makes it possible to see the object.

Book

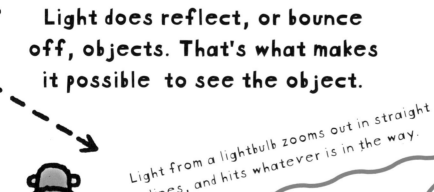

Light from a lightbulb zooms out in straight lines, and hits whatever is in the way.

For example, you can see your book because some light rays bounce off it and into your eyes.

Lightbulb

Eye

Soaking up light

But surfaces don't reflect ALL the light that hits them. They also absorb, or soak up, some of it. Even a mirror absorbs a bit of light.

All objects are made up of tiny **particles** called **atoms**. The light energy absorbed by an object makes the atoms in it move faster, heating it up slightly. Because the energy has changed from light energy to heat energy, the light disappears.

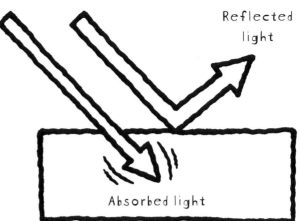

Reflected light

Absorbed light

Lights out!

When you turn off your light, the last rays of light bounce around the room. Each time they hit a surface, more light gets soaked up, until it's all gone.

But light travels VERY fast, at a super-speedy...

186,000 miles per second!
(300,000 km per second)

All of this bouncing around happens in the tiniest blink of an eye—and then you're in the dark!

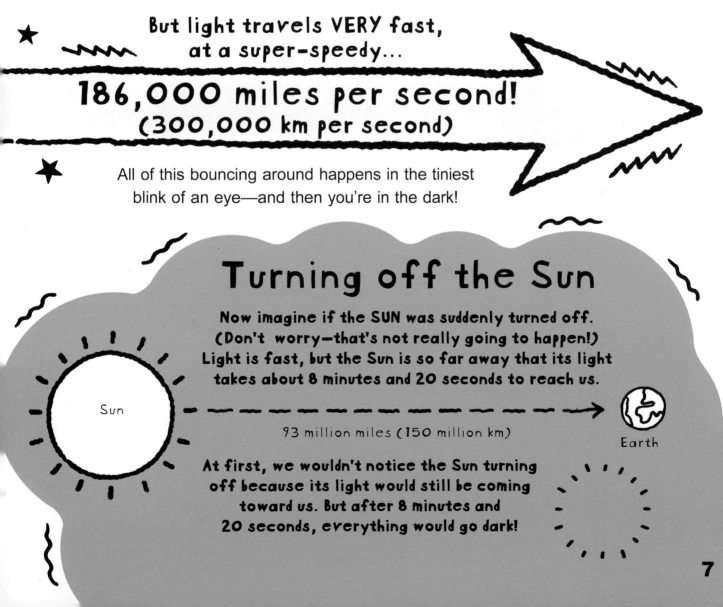

Turning off the Sun

Now imagine if the SUN was suddenly turned off. (Don't worry—that's not really going to happen!) Light is fast, but the Sun is so far away that its light takes about 8 minutes and 20 seconds to reach us.

Sun

93 million miles (150 million km)

Earth

At first, we wouldn't notice the Sun turning off because its light would still be coming toward us. But after 8 minutes and 20 seconds, everything would go dark!

Why does a mirror show things backwards?

Write HELLO! on a piece of paper and hold it up to a mirror. The word will look backwards in the mirror, like this:

When you look in a mirror, you see a flipped version of yourself.

Try it!

Maggie the cat

What Maggie sees in the mirror.

Eyepatch on right eye

Eyepatch on left eye

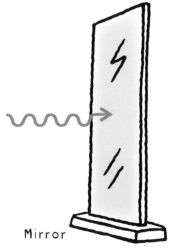

Mirror

How does this work?

Also why do mirrors only flip things left to right, and not upside down? People are often puzzled by this, but the answer is simple: mirrors don't flip anything! When rays of light hit a mirror, they bounce right off.

Mirror

If you're standing right in front of a mirror, it will reflect you right back, like this:

Your head is at the top, and your feet are at the bottom.

Your right arm is on the right side in the mirror.

Your right side is on the right side in the mirror.

Light rays

No flipping!

It's the same with writing in the mirror.

So why does it look flipped?!

HELLO OTHER ME!

To face the mirror, you have to flip yourself around.
Imagine if there were two of you.

To look at your double, you would face them.

If you wanted to see them in the mirror, they'd have to turn around and face away from you and look at the mirror. So they would flip left-to-right.

When you hold writing up to the mirror, you have turned it around so that it faces the mirror. You've flipped it. The mirror just reflects what's there.

Why does the Moon shine?

On a clear night, you can often see the Moon shining brightly, especially when it's full. In fact, long ago, before streetlights were invented, people often used the light of the Moon to find their way.

But the Moon is NOT a light source. It doesn't actually glow or give off light at all! What we call moonlight is really sunlight. Light from the Sun hits the Moon and is reflected onto Earth. The Moon acts like a big mirror in the sky.

Sun

Sunlight

Moon

Earth

Reflected light

Why does the Moon change shape?

As you've probably noticed, the Moon looks different from one day to the next.

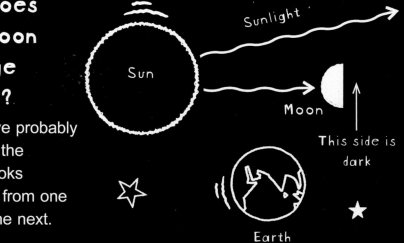

Sun

Sunlight

Moon

This side is dark

Earth

How does THAT work???

Wherever the Moon is, sunlight falls on it, lighting up one side of it. Because light travels in straight lines, the Sun can't light up the other side.

We see the Moon from different angles as it **orbits** around Earth. For example, in this picture the Moon is moving toward the Sun.

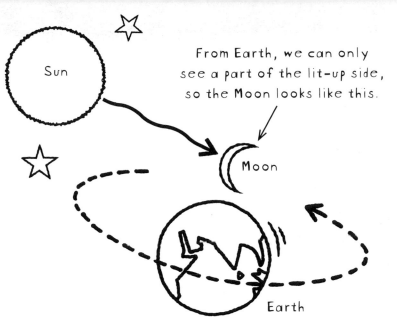

Sun

From Earth, we can only see a part of the lit-up side, so the Moon looks like this.

Moon

Earth

Round and round

The Moon takes almost a month to orbit the Earth. In that time, it appears to change from full to invisible and back again.

The phases of the Moon:

New Moon | Waxing crescent | First Quarter | Waxing gibbous | Full Moon | Waning gibbous | Last Quarter | Waning crescent

And did you know that...

The planets don't shine either?! In the night sky, planets seem to shine just like stars. But they don't really.

Stars are light sources and give off their own light energy. Planets are just big balls of rock, liquid, ice, or gas. Like the Moon, they don't shine. They just reflect the Sun's light.

Star

Planet

Saturn is mostly made of gas, with rings of ice and rock.

Mars is made of reddish-colored rock.

I'M QUITE CHILLY YOU KNOW!

How can your shadow be taller than you?

Sometimes your shadow is short and sometimes it's really long! If you've ever walked under a streetlight at night, you might even have seen your shadow growing as you move along the street.

Looooong shadow

Straight lines

Shadows happen because light rays travel in straight lines.

Light shines from a light source.

When it hits an object that isn't **transparent**, the light bounces off the object or gets absorbed into it.

Other light rays travel in straight lines past the object. They can't curve around behind it.

Shadow

Light can't reach the area behind the object. This is the object's shadow.

The long and the short of it

The length of your shadow on the ground depends on where the light source is compared to the ground.

Sun high in the sky

Light rays

Shorter shadow

Sun low in the sky

Light rays

Longer shadow

When the light source is lower, the light has to travel farther to get past you. Your shadow looks stretched out.

Look at this person!

His shadow is so short, it's right underneath him.

If your shadow is directly under you, it means the Sun is directly above your head, right in the middle of the sky. This can only happen in places that are on or near the **equator**, because the equator is in line with the Sun.

Sun

Longer shadows

Shorter shadows

Earth

Equator

Longer shadows

How do binoculars make things look closer?

Look through a pair of binoculars at a bird nest at the other end of the street, and you'll see the bird and its nest just as if they were right in front of you!

Sshh.... That's why birdwatchers use binoculars to watch birds. They can stay far away and not disturb the birds.

But HOW does that happen?

You know how light travels in straight lines? Well, it's actually a BIT more complicated than that. Light can actually change direction. For example, when a light ray hits a mirror or other surface, it is reflected and bounces off.

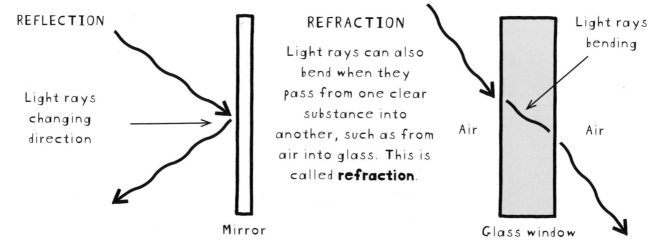

REFLECTION

Light rays changing direction

Mirror

REFRACTION

Light rays can also bend when they pass from one clear substance into another, such as from air into glass. This is called **refraction**.

Light rays bending

Air

Air

Glass window

Through a lens

Binoculars work by refracting light rays using **lenses**, which are special curved pieces of glass.

Light rays

Eye

Retina

Lens inside a pair of binoculars.

Bird

How the bird appears.

The lens bends the light rays inward. This makes a bigger image on the **retina** at the back of the eye, so the bird looks bigger. It also appears to be closer since things look bigger when they are closer up.

Take a closer look!

We use lenses in lots of devices and inventions to make things look closer or clearer.

HELLO!

Magnifying glass

Telescope

Microscope

Make glass disappear!

Ask an adult for help with this refraction experiment. You need a glass bowl or jug, a small glass, and some baby oil.

① Put the small glass into the jug or bowl.

② Pour in enough baby oil to cover it.

③ The small glass should vanish!

Some substances refract light more than others. Glass and oil are very similar in how much they refract light. When the glass is in the oil, light rays pass through them both without bending much at all, making the small glass very hard to see.

15

Where do the stars go in the daytime?

On a dark, clear night, the sky is full of stars. In the daytime, you can't see them, but they haven't gone anywhere. They're still there!

When you look up at the sky on a sunny day, you are still looking at stars. Earth is surrounded by stars in all directions.

You just can't see them!

But why?

The Sun is a star just like all the other stars. But it's much, much closer to Earth. The Sun is a mind-boggling 93 million miles (150 million km) away, but the nearest stars are over 24.85 trillion miles (40 trillion km) away. That's why the stars look much smaller and fainter to us than the Sun.

Night skies...

At night, a small, faint point of light is easy to see in the dark.

Bright skies...

During the daytime, the huge, bright Sun is in the sky. It's so bright, it lights up the rest of the sky, too. Sunlight is made up of all colors. But when it hits the particles in Earth's atmosphere, the colors in the light scatter in all directions. Blue light scatters the easiest, which is why the sky looks blue to us.

Sun

Air particles in the atmosphere

The sky is lit up so much brighter than the light from the stars that the stars don't show up.

Light in your eyes

Your eyes play a part in this, too.

In bright light, your **pupils** shrink to let in less light, so that your eyes don't get damaged.

In dim light or darkness, your pupils open up to let in more light.

Shut the curtains!

In the same way, it's hard to see a tiny candle flame in a bright room. But you can see the flame clearly if you shut the curtains and make the room dark.

At night, your eyes let in more light, making them more sensitive to the twinkly starlight.

What makes things different colors?

What color is this T-shirt?
Yellow, of course!

Or IS it?

Have you ever wondered why some things are yellow, and others are pink, orange, or black? It's all to do with how light reflects off them.

So what does "being yellow" really mean?

Colors of light

Light rays travel through space in the form of a form of energy called electromagnetic waves. These waves have a wavelength.

Crest

Wavelength

Trough

The wavelength is the length of one complete wave.

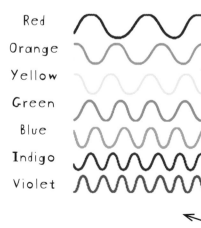

Red
Orange
Yellow
Green
Blue
Indigo
Violet

A spectrum of colors

All light doesn't have the same wavelength. In fact, it comes in many different wavelengths. We see these different wavelengths as a spectrum, or range, of colors. You can see this range in a rainbow. Red light has the longest wavelength, and violet has the shortest. The others are in between.

These colors are **visible light**, or light we can see with our eyes.

Why are there seven colors?

There aren't really only seven colors. There are actually many colors. They are made by combining the seven colors in different ways.

LOOKS LIKE SEVEN TO ME!

It was the famous scientist Isaac Newton (1643–1727) who divided the spectrum into seven colors and named them.

Now back to the T-shirt!

How can an object or surface be a color? Light from the Sun or a lightbulb is made of all the wavelengths mixed together. We see this complete mixture as white light.

Sun

Eye

Objects and surfaces reflect some light, but they also absorb some of it.

A surface that looks yellow, such as this T-shirt, has absorbed every other color wavelength...

...but has reflected yellow. So yellow is what you see!

A white object reflects all the wavelengths, so we see white light.

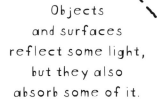

A black object soaks up almost all the wavelengths, so it looks dark.

Some things reflect a combination of wavelengths, such as this brown bear.

Colors in the dark 🌙

In the dark it's hard to see colors. Everything looks grayish. You can only see colors properly if white light is shining on things. Without light, nothing really has a color!

Why can't you reach the end of a rainbow?

This is just one of the many mysteries of rainbows. Why can't you find the end of the rainbow? According to **legend**, there's supposed to be a pot of gold there.

And why do rainbows happen anyway?

Color and sunshine

Rainbow colors come from the Sun. Bright white sunlight contains all the different wavelengths, or colors, of visible light (see pages 18–19).

In a raindrop

When sunlight shines into a raindrop, the light rays are reflected and refracted, making them bend.

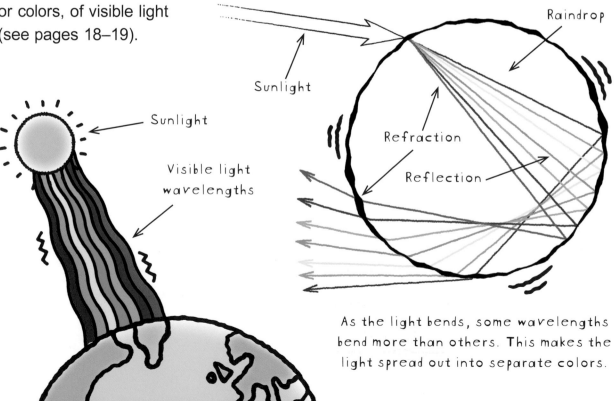

Sunlight

Visible light wavelengths

Sunlight

Raindrop

Refraction

Reflection

As the light bends, some wavelengths bend more than others. This makes the light spread out into separate colors.

Seeing the rainbow

When you look at a rainbow, you're looking at a sky full of many tiny raindrops, with the Sun shining on them from behind you.

42°

The rainbow light shines out of each drop at a 42° angle from the sunlight shining in.

You only see a rainbow if you are at exactly the right distance for this light to reflect back to your eyes.

This is why you can never see the end of a rainbow. You can only see it when the angle and the distance are just right.

Rainbows are round!

When you're on the ground, rainbows usually look like an arc or semicircle. But if the ground wasn't in the way, the rainbow would be a whole circle.

People sometimes spot circular rainbows from aircraft.

How does light get inside your eyes?

Our planet is bathed in light from the Sun, Moon, and stars. It constantly bounces around, reflecting off objects and surfaces.

Being able to detect light is very useful. It means we can sense where things are—even faraway things—as long as there's some light coming from them. So, over time, animals have **evolved** different kinds of eyes to see better.

Hammerhead shark

Eyes on side of head

Mammals, birds, lizards, and fish tend to have two eyes.

Huge eyes

Bush baby

Spiders have up to eight eyes.

Eyes

Jumping spider

This scallop has dozens of eyes!

The simplest eyes are just spots. Creatures with these eyes can only sense light or tell day and night apart.

MUST BE BEDTIME!

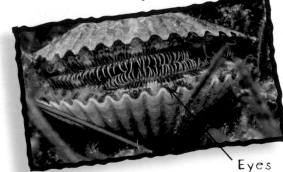

Eyes

Eye spots

Flatworm

Human eyes

Over time, many animals, including humans, have developed quite **complex** eyes. They let light right inside them and capture a sharp image of the world—just like a camera. (Actually, it's cameras that are like eyes. Eyes were here first!)

Incoming!

Here is what happens when light enters your eyes:

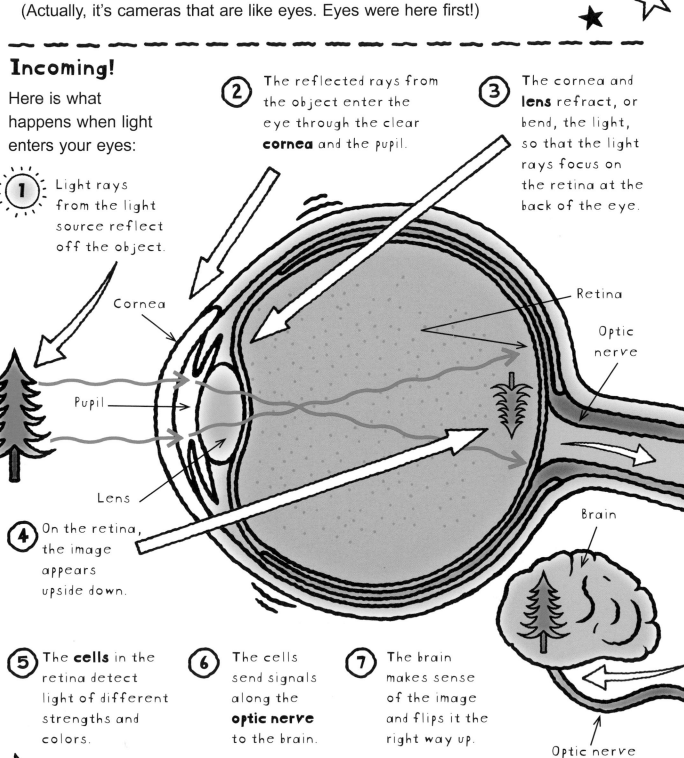

1 Light rays from the light source reflect off the object.

2 The reflected rays from the object enter the eye through the clear **cornea** and the pupil.

3 The cornea and **lens** refract, or bend, the light, so that the light rays focus on the retina at the back of the eye.

Cornea

Pupil

Lens

Retina

Optic nerve

Brain

Optic nerve

4 On the retina, the image appears upside down.

5 The **cells** in the retina detect light of different strengths and colors.

6 The cells send signals along the **optic nerve** to the brain.

7 The brain makes sense of the image and flips it the right way up.

How can an X-ray see through you?

OUCH!

If you've ever broken a bone, you might have seen something a bit spooky—a photo of your own skeleton inside your body!

An **X-ray** is a type of photograph. But instead of using the normal light we can see, it's made using a different type of light: X-rays!

Invisible light

That's right! There's more to light than meets the eye!

Invisible light

Invisible light

Visible light

There's visible light, with its spectrum of different wavelengths and colors...

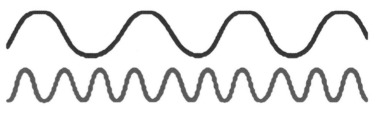

...and there are many more types of light, with longer or shorter wavelengths.

These are all the same type of waves, known as electromagnetic waves. They behave in the same way and travel at the same (incredibly fast) speed. But our eyes can only see a short range of wavelengths, which we call visible light. The others are invisible to the eye.

The electromagnetic spectrum

This chart shows the electromagnetic spectrum, or the whole range of electromagnetic waves, from the shortest to the longest.
They include X-rays, microwaves, and **radio waves**.

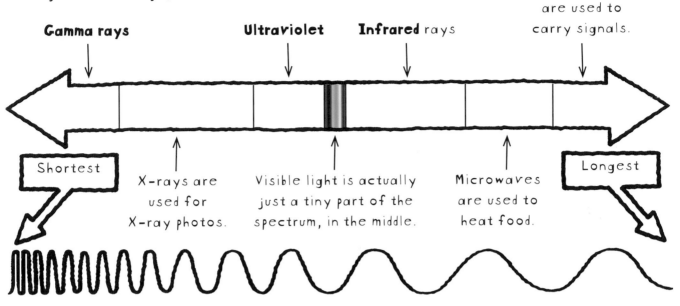

Gamma rays

Ultraviolet

Infrared rays

Radio waves are used to carry signals.

Shortest

X-rays are used for X-ray photos.

Visible light is actually just a tiny part of the spectrum, in the middle.

Microwaves are used to heat food.

Longest

X-rays

X-rays are a type of shorter electromagnetic wave. They can pass through some objects that block visible light. That's how they can look inside you.

An X-ray machine zaps X-rays through your body. They can shine through some body parts, such as muscle, but not bone.

A screen detects the rays that come through, resulting in an image.

Why X?

X MARKS THE SPOT.

German scientist Wilhelm Röntgen (1845–1923) discovered X-rays in 1895, but he wasn't sure what they were. He named them X-rays because in math, "X" means something unknown. The name stuck!

Is an invisibility cloak possible?

In the Harry Potter stories, Harry can make himself disappear using his amazing invisibility cloak. Most of us would love to be able to turn invisible—but could we really make an invisibility cloak?

Visible

Invisible!

Harry Potter's cloak works using magic, which is cheating! To make an invisibility cloak that works in the real world, we have to use science.

Scientists are actually trying to do it, and they've come up with a few brilliant ideas...

① Bend the light around

This method uses lenses to refract and bend light around an object. When you look at the object, you see the light coming from behind it, so it looks as if it's not there.

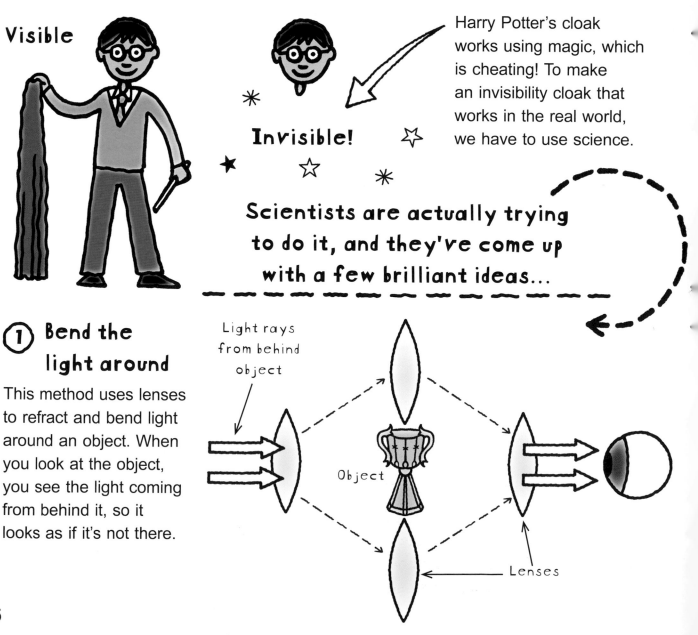

Light rays from behind object

Object

Lenses

② Direct the light around

This is similar to method 1, but you curve the light around the object by sending it along tiny **fiber-optic cables**.

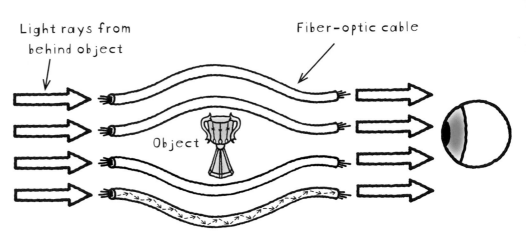

Light rays from behind object

Fiber-optic cable

Object

Light reflects off the inside of a fiber-optic cable.

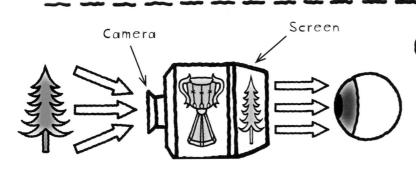

Camera

Screen

③ Project the background

This device has a camera at the back and a screen at the front. The camera films what's behind the object and puts it on the screen.

④ Shine the light through

This device catches the light rays that shine at the object, and turns them into a different kind of ray that can pass through the object, such as an X-ray. Then, on the other side, it turns them back into visible light again, making the object seem transparent.

Visible light rays

Rays that can pass through the object

Visible light rays

So where can I get one?!

Sadly, Harry-Potter-style cloaks aren't quite ready yet. So far, scientists have only managed to make very small objects invisible for a short time, if they stay still.

I'M RIGHT HERE!

Quick-fire questions

How can light let us see back in time?

Imagine an object in space is a hundred **light years** away. When we look at it, we see light that has taken a hundred years to reach us. So the light set off from the object a hundred years ago, and, by the time it reaches us, we are seeing it as it was a hundred years ago!

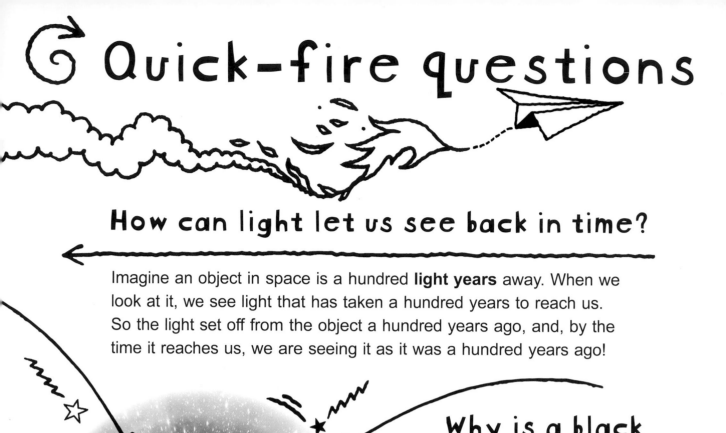

Why is a black hole black?

Black holes are space objects that have very powerful gravity. They are so strong they can even suck in light. If light rays get close enough to a black hole, they get sucked in and can't escape. So you can never see light shining or reflecting from a black hole, and it looks completely dark.

Why does sunlight feel warm?

As well as visible light, sunlight contains infrared light, which has a slightly longer wavelength than red visible light. Your skin absorbs the infrared light. In your body, the wave energy makes **molecules** in your skin move faster, which you feel as heat.

Why are some people color-blind?

Our eyes see colors using cells in the retina called **cone cells**. Different cone cells are sensitive to different colors, and you can tell what color something is by which combinations of cones it triggers. In color-blind people, some of the cone cells don't work properly, so it's hard for them to see some colors, or to tell some colors apart from each other.

Why do people's legs look shorter in a swimming pool?

This illusion is because of refraction. Light coming from your legs refracts and bends as it leaves the water surface and enters the air. To your eyes, the bent rays of light look as if they have come from higher up than they really have, so legs look shortened. This effect can also make water look shallower than it really is.

How do glow-in-the dark stars work?

Glow-in-the-dark ceiling stars, clothes, and toys contain chemicals called **phosphors**. When light shines on them, they absorb it, store it, and then release it again slowly. So if light shines on an item with phosphors during the day, it will keep glowing with light for a while after the lights are turned off.

Glossary

atoms The smallest pieces that make up everything in the world

black holes Tiny, extremely dense points in space with very powerful gravity

cells Units made up of molecules that make up living things

chemical A substance that cannot be broken down into different parts

complex Not easy to learn or understand

cone cells Cells in the retina at the back of the eye that detect colors of light

cornea The clear, curved window covering the pupil at the front of the eyeball

electromagnetic wave A type of energy wave that includes visible light, X-rays, radio waves, and several others

energy The power to make things happen or do work

equator An imaginary line around the middle of Earth

evolved Changed over time, especially living things

fiber-optic cable A very thin, flexible glass tube that can carry light along inside it

gamma rays High-energy electromagnetic waves with a very short wavelength

gravity A force that pulls all objects toward each other

infrared A type of electromagnetic wave with a wavelength slightly longer than visible light

legend A traditional story that is usually considered to be untrue

lens (in the eye) A clear part of the eye just behind the pupil, which helps to focus light rays on the retina

lenses (devices) Pieces of clear material such as glass, shaped to make light refract and bend

light rays Lines of light, used in diagrams to show the direction light is traveling in

light year The distance light travels in one year

mammals Types of warm-blooded animals that feed their babies on milk

microwaves Electromagnetic waves with a wavelength longer than visible light

molecules Units made up of atoms

optic nerve A bundle of nerves that carry information from the eyeball to the brain

orbits To circle around another object, for example when the Moon orbits Earth

particles Units that make up atoms

phase A period or stage in a process of change

phosphors Chemicals that can absorb light energy and then release it by glowing

pupils The small round openings at the front of the eyeballs that let light in

radio waves Electromagnetic waves with a wavelength much longer than visible light

refraction The way light rays can bend as they pass from one transparent substance into another

retina A layer of light-detecting cells inside the back of the eyeball

transparent Describes something that allows light to pass through it, making it see-through

ultraviolet (UV) An electromagnetic wave with a wavelength slightly shorter than visible light

visible light The range of electromagnetic waves that we see as light, including the spectrum of colors from violet to red

X-rays Electromagnetic waves with a wavelength shorter than visible light

Learning More

Books

Chatterton, Crystal. *Awesome Science Experiments for Kids.* Rockridge Press, 2018.

Claybourne, Anna. *Recreate Discoveries about Light.* Crabtree Publishing, 2018.

Johnson, Robin. *The Science of Light Waves.* Crabtree Publishing, 2017.

Kenney, Karen Latchana. *Sound and Light Waves Investigations.* Lerner Publications, 2017.

Websites

www.stevespanglerscience.com/lab/categories/experiments/light-and-sound/
Lots of light and sound experiments to try out.

www.dkfindout.com/us/science/light/
Light facts, photos, and a fun quiz.

www.sciencekids.co.nz/light.html
Light facts, games, and amazing videos.

www.sciencelearn.org.nz/image_maps/63-the-electromagnetic-spectrum
All about the electromagnetic spectrum.

https://ocean.si.edu/ocean-life/fish/bioluminescent-animals-photo-gallery
Photo gallery of animals that glow with their own light.

Index

A
animal eyes 22, 23

B
binoculars 14, 15
black holes 28

C
color 17, 18, 19, 20, 23,
  24, 29
color blindness 29
color spectrum 18, 19, 24
cone cells 29
cornea 23

E
electromagnetic waves 5,
  18, 24, 25
energy 4–5, 6, 7, 11, 18,
  28
equator 13
eyes 4, 6, 15, 17, 18, 19,
  21, 22–23, 24, 29

G
gamma rays 25
gravity 5, 28

I
infrared 25, 28
invisibility 15, 26–27
invisible light 24, 25

L
lenses 15, 23, 26
lightbulbs 4, 5, 6, 19
light rays 5, 6, 7, 8, 9, 12,
  13, 14, 15, 18, 20, 23, 26,
  27, 28, 29

M
microwaves 25
mirrors 7, 8, 9, 10, 14
Moon 10–11, 22

N
Newton, Isaac 19

P
phosphors 29
photons 5
planets 11
pupils 17, 23

R
radio waves 25
rainbows 18, 20–21
raindrops 20–21
reflection 6, 7, 9, 10, 11,
  14, 18, 19, 20, 21, 22, 23,
  27, 28
refraction 14, 15, 20, 23,
  26, 29
retina 15, 23, 29
Röntgen, Wilhelm 25

S
shadows 12–13
stars 4, 11, 16, 17, 22
Sun 4, 7, 10–11, 13, 16,
  17, 19, 20, 21, 22, 28

U
ultraviolet 25

V
visible light 18, 20, 24, 25,
  27, 28

W
white light 19, 20

X
X-rays 24–25, 27